Stuttgart

The City between Woods and Vineyards -
Partner of the World

With an Introduction by the
Lord Mayor Dr. Arnulf Klett

PUBLISHERS DIE SCHOENEN BUECHER
DR. WOLF STRACHE STUTTGART

© Copyright by Publishers Die Schoenen Buecher

Dr. Wolf Strache, Stuttgart

Printed in Germany · All rights reserved

Twelfth revised edition

"Die Schoenen Buecher", Series D "German Towns" · Volume 1

Edited by Dr. Wolf Strache

All photographs by Dr. Wolf Strache

Cover by Armin Schraft, Stuttgart-Botnang

Production by Bros. Rath, Stuttgart-Vaihingen

JSNB 3-7956-0046-4

City Between Woods and Vineyards — Partner of the World

There can hardly be another large German city which enjoys such a unique location as Stuttgart. Surrounded by gentle hills, on whose slopes vines and orchards flourish, the city rests in the valley basin; in all directions the residential areas and suburbs clamber up the hills and even descend into the neighbouring valleys so that, in the true sense of the word, one can say that the city has grown up-hill and down dale.

In the centre of the city the old heart of the former Residence has been retained or tastefully restored, once again giving the impression of unity: the venerable Cathedral, the Old Castle with its mighty towers and the magnificent Arcades, the square around the Schiller Monument with the Old Chancery and the New Castle which has once again been restored to its former splendour. The Castle Square with the Jubilee Column and the Royal Palace with its colonnade is the green focal point of the city. Only a few yards away from the bustling traffic a new park has been created out of the former palace grounds. The "Kleine Haus" of the State Theatre and the Landtagsgebäude, where the Diet meets, all blend harmoniously into the spacious grounds of the Palace Gardens.

Somebody once said that Stuttgart would "drown in wine" if its citizens had to drink all the wine themselves. Many of the vineyards have vanished in recent times, but the visitor is still often amazed to see well-cultivated vineyards immediately above the Main Station and on countless other slopes around the city. Down below, however, the industrious city with its approximate 630,000 inhabitants spreads out. Here, day and night, such world-famous firms as Daimler Benz, Porsche, Bosch, Zeiss-Ikon, Berger, Bleyle, Hudson, Standard-Elektrik and many others, not forgetting the countless publishing houses, are at work. These are names and products known all over the world, but who is aware – abroad or even in Germany – that Stuttgart also has many, highly productive mineral springs which fill refreshing pools for thousands of visitors on warm summer days. Who is familiar with the secluded beauty of the many hundred steps and steep paths which lead up on all sides of the city? Of the many green parks the most important, the Killesberg, is probably known to many people, as it was the core of the Federal Horticultural Show in 1961. But there are many small ones, often known only to local inhabitants. Worth mentioning ar the Weissenburg Park with its fine view,

3

the idyllic Hoppenlau Cemetery, the gardens of the Villa Berg, the charming Uhlandshöhe, the new park grounds around the Assembly House, and then one should not forget the wooded areas which cover the hills all around the sunny city.

One can best get an impression of the city nestling in its beautiful surroundings if one ascends to the platform of the Television Tower which has become a new landmark of the city since it was built in 1956. This 700-foot-high masterpiece of technology has justly taken its place alongside the other ancient symbols of the city, the Cathedral and the Schiller Monument, to which it owes its historical fame.

In the meantime, of course, a number of other surprising edifices have been added to the list: the Stuttgart Harbour, which has exceeded all expectations in rapidly becoming an important factor in the economic life of the city, the reconstruction of the city centre which, through the creation of the "Kleiner Schlossplatz", and Underground and tram-network and many tunnelled road junctions, has been decicively modernized, and finally the start of construction work on the commutor railway which is planned to create in the near future a rapid means of communication between all outlying districts and the city.

One cannot hope to get to know Stuttgart and all its delightful attractions in a few hours. It takes time and patience to become familiar with the city. Anyone who takes the trouble to look through its busy streets and then stroll along the quiet paths will not fail to appreciate some of the city's unique atmosphere.

Klett

Lord Mayor

17 The Television Tower

Still a long way off, one catches sight of Stuttgart's new landmark, the slim column of the Television Tower. The over 700-foot-high column with the cage — several stories high — plus the red and white antenna, can be seen from the Autobahn and over all the hills around the city. From the two platforms, about 490 foot high, one obtains a wonderful panorama of all Stuttgart with its suburbs and residential areas on the slopes, and even as far north as Asperg and as far south as the Swabian Jura. On television every evening its image is transmitted as the landmark of modern Stuttgart. Since its construction in 1954–1956 it has been imitated all over the world from Moscow to Tokyo. Framed between the flags of friendly nations it can be taken as a new symbol for the city: partner of the world.

18/19 The City Centre

From the Eugenplatz one can see the city centre with the Old and New Castles, the Cathedral and Town Hall, the prominent towers of the Main Station and the Daily Newspaper – not visible in the picture — complete the panorama. All around wooded slopes and vineyards frame the city with a green background. The old saying about the "city between woods and vineyards" is still valid.

20 The Old Castle

With its mighty towers the Old Castle once again dominates the city centre. It was originally constructed as a fortress with a moat, but in 1553 Herzog Christoph replanned it as a Renaissance palace. A serious fire in 1931 and then bomb damage in 1944 destroyed large sections of this building, almost down to the foundations. With great care and devotion the restauration work has only recently been completed.

21 Schiller Square and Collegiate Church

The Schillerplatz, with the double-towered Cathedral and the Schiller Monument by Thorwaldsen, is certainly one of the most attractive and secluded squares in Germany. The oldest part of the Cathedral was built around 1175, the chancel was added in 1350, and the nave and the west tower were completed at the beginning of the 16th century. The broad gable end of the neighbouring "Fruchtkasten" is a work of the architect Heinrich Schickhardt. The building in which wine was pressed in former days now accommodates the Lapidarium. The "Prinzenbau", the Old Chancery and Old Castle join up this venerable square with the other side. Somewhat further away, the tower of the

Town Hall rise above the roof tops. On some days of the week the flower market, which takes place on the square, recalls some of the romance of earlier times.

<table>
<tr><td>22</td><td>In the Wurtemberg
State Museum</td></tr>
<tr><td>23</td><td>Courtyard
of the Old Castle</td></tr>
</table>

On completion of the construction work the Old Castle regained not only its historical appearance, but was also able to provide ideal accommodation for the selection of the Wurtemberg State Museum which was then arranged in a new and more impressive way. In an engaging manner related groups of medieaval and post-medieaval art are placed adjacent to one another, for example, a wooden "cross bearer" of the late 15th century and the large picture of the Passion of Christ from the Zwiefalten Monastery. Above the inner courtyards of the Castle with its 3-storey arcades one can catch sight of the towers of the nearby Cathedral.

24/
25 Schlossplatz with
    Towers of the Town

From the roof terrace of a high office building one can gaze over the chestnut trees in Castle Square and see all the important higher buildings in the city. Beside the thick towers of the Old Castle rises the slender Jubilee Column; to the right of this one can recognize the light coloured building of the Town Hall and the Tagblatt-Turm (Daily Newspaper), and then somewhat to the side come the towers of the Cathedral.

26 Crucifixion Group
    Outside the
    St. Leonhard Church

In the midst of the busy traffic on the Hauptstätter Street stands the Gothic Church of St. Leonhard, which was commenced before 1408, and also the expressive Crucifixion Group created by the sculptor Hans Seyfer in 1501. The original piece of sculpture, a bequest made by Jacob der Ältere Walther, surnamed Kühorn, and his wife, is to be found today in the nave of the Hospitalkirche. The excellent copy dating from 1891 affords the square beside the Leonhardskirche a unique accent, just like the neighbouring Nachtwächterbrunnen (Watchman's Fountain) in the Leonhardsplatz which forms a charming contrast to the high buildings and the parking building.

27 Market Square
    with Collegiate Church

Narrow-fronted shops in differing pastel shades surround the Stuttgart market place and convey a faint impression of the once so romantic picture which the rows of timber-framed houses must have presented. Above the flat roof tops rise the towers of the Cathedral.

28 Flower Market and Town Hall

At various times of the day a chime of bells can be heard over the Market Place. Here, and on the nearby Schillerplatz, a market, which takes place three times a week, which lends colour to the street scene. The light-coloured New Town Hall designed by the architects Schmohl and Stohrer was constructed between the years 1953 – 56 to replace the Old Town Hall which was destroyed during the war. Beneath the tower, which can be seen a great distance away, are located the conference room and various representative offices, and annexed to this are broad wings.

29 Schulstrasse

One of the busiest shopping streets in the city centre is the Schulstrasse which connects up the Market Place with the lower section of the Königstrasse. It is reserved for pedestrians, and the entire zone is delightfully linked up by high-level walks and stairs.

30 Kleiner Schlossplatz
31 Café at Kleiner Schlossplatz

With the creation of the Kleiner Schlossplatz the city centre received a further attractive architectural note: on top of the tunnel by means of which the Federal Highway 27 cuts under the city centre – one has built, as a sort of enormous "lid", the Square which now boasts multi-storeyed office blocks and low shops. Cafés and restaurants, boutiques and fountains add colourful life to the severe lines of the concrete architecture. At the top of a wide escalator leading up from the lower Schlossplatz there is a piece of sculpture which the Stuttgart artist Hajek created especially for the Kleiner Schlossplatz. Once or twice a year the Square is transformed into an enormous stage when, to the accompaniment of music and fortified with fried sausages and "Laugenbretzeln" artists and many thousands of visitors join in the "Grosse Fest am Kleinen Schlossplatz" and the "Schwäbische Sonntag".

32 Königsbau in the Castle Square

Fountains of gushing water and carefully tended flower beds have helped to make the Schlossplatz a friendly oasis in the heart of the city. Along its west side stretches the functional Königsbau with its colonnade and the countless shops. It was built between 1857–60 and after the war it was restored to its original form. On one side it is joined by the Kleiner Schlossplatz which augments the "classical" shopping arcade through its expensive modern architecture.

In the grounds of the Upper Castle Gardens with the asymmetrically shaped lake stands the magnificent Opera House, the so-called "Grosses Haus" of the Wurtemberg State Theatre; when it was opened in 1912 it was one of the most modern theatre buildings of that time. With its famous opera and ballet productions it has made a name for itself amongst the leading international stages.

The Schlossplatz (Castle Square) and the Castle Gardens are the green and festive focal points of the city and form at the same time the beginning of a chain of park-like grounds which extend down to the river Neckar, to the Rosenstein Castle and to the Wilhelma. The baroque castle, built between 1746–1807 and restored in 1964 borders off the Castle Courtyard and also the Castle Square with its central tract and the side wings. The famous Weisser Saal is used when Stuttgart has important guests to receive. The Castle Garden with its sculptures, its gay fountains and ponds is open to all the citizens and guests of the city.

Beside the "Theatersee" stands the new playhouse, the so-called "Kleines Haus" of the Wurtemberg State Theatre. The square in front of the foyer is lent an interesting accent by the metal sculpture by Bertoni.

The Castle Gardens extend from the city centre to Cannstatt and serves as a large park with a wide variety of recreational and entertainment facilities. Out-door chess and "boule", cafés and milk-bars are at the disposal of walkers. Over hammered metal plates the water splashes down into the fountain pool of the Castle Gardens. At the edge of the gardens there still stands the historical remnants of the former Royal Summer House, a relic of almost forgotten bombastic architecture.

The over 180-foot-high tower of the Main Station stands sentinel over the busy Königstrasse and the city centre. The Stuttgart Station, designed by Professor Bonatz in 1914 and completed in 1927 is still regarded as a classical example of a modern utility building.

39	Cross-Roads Charlottenplatz	In the course of the construction of the Underground the important traffic intersection Charlottenstrasse – Konrad Adenauer-Strasse was replanned on a large scale and adapted to the needs of modern traffic. The motor traffic along the Neckarstrasse–Hauptstätter Strasse now flows uninterrupted through a tunnel. As the streams of traffic meet they are separated and joined up again in a clear and orderly fashion. Trams pass underneath the Square at two interconnected levels and thus no longer obstruct the motor traffic. From the high building in the Charlottenplatz one can get a good overall view of the junction and the adjoining public buildings: New Castle, Landtag and State Theatre, State Archive and State Library.
40/ 41	Charlottenplatz, Underground Tramway	The Charlottenplatz gives one an idea of what the Stuttgart of the future will look like. The movement of pedestrians and vehicles take place at several subterranean levels. The intersection of the Underground lines can be reached either via escalators or gently sloping walks, and the street exit and shopping centres are also incoporated in the system. On the surface there is space for parking-buildings, offices and new municipal projects which, within the next few years, will give the region around the Hauptstätter Street a new, functional appearance.
42	Office Buildings at the Friedrichstrasse	Multi-storey offices and administrative buildings, the College of Science and Technology, hotels and airline agencies are typical of the most important streets which — like the Friedrichstrasse in this photo — cut a broad path into the city. From year to year the picture is changing rapidly: familiar sights are vanishing and new, tall building are shooting up.
43	Hofbräu Corner and Tagblatt Skyscraper	Also the intersection of the upper part of Königstrasse with the Eberhard- and Marientrasse and the adjoining area of the Rotebühlplatz have undergone considerable change. Beneath the surrounding buildings — the tower of the Stuttgart Newspaper, Kaufhaus C & A Brenninkmeyer, Kaufhaus Merkur, Hofbräueck and Wullehaus – an extensive subterranean project is in progress which envisages within the next few years an intersection at several levels of the Underground and the commuter railway. Even today the tramway network in Stuttgart transports 113 million passengers in a year, and the bus lines an

additional 25 million. The commuter railway (called the "S-Bahn"), the first section of which will connect up the Main Station with Vaihingen via the Rotebühlplatz, is intended to ease the load on local traffic facilities and on completion will probably represent the largest compound traffic network in the Federal Republic.

44/
45   In front of the
     Concert Hall

Both flights of stairs lead up to the square in front of the Liederhalle, the walls of which are gaily decorated with abstract sculpture and multicoloured mosaics. The extensive edifice with its protruding arches, displacement of areas and many overlapping sections constantly alters its silhouette when one walks around it. The architectural experience is even more surprising when one enters the Concert Hall through the light foyer. Here the principles of modern accoustics have been applied in conjunction with new arrangements of the orchestra and auditorium. Colour and interesting structural forms have been introduced to the Hall by the use of unusual materials applied in a wide variety of ways.

46   College buildings
     of the University
47   The New University
     Buildings at Pfaffenwald

With its numerous colleges the University of Stuttgart ranks after Berlin, Frankfurt and Munich (and together with Hanover and Cologne) as one of the largest in the Federal Republic. It possesses institutes, lecture rooms and libraries in three central points of the town – in the city on the site of the former College of Science and Technology, the two most impressive structures being the high twin buildings and the nearby library – in the recently opened university precincts at Pfaffenwald, where abstract sculpture takes its place amongst the numerous new buildings — and in Hohenheim which originally commenced with the Agricultural College accommodated in the Castle. In addition there is the State Academy of Fine Art, the State Academy of Music and the Teachers' Training College.

48   Gottlieb-Daimler-
     High School

In 1966 one of the most modern school buildings in the Federal Republic, the Gottlieb-Daimler-Gymnasium in Bad Cannstatt, was inaugurated. The ideally arranged classrooms have been supplemented by terraces at various roof levels for use during the break time. Stuttgart has a total of 160 state schools, including 40 secondary schools, as well as 17 special schools. The number of school children in Stuttgart is 100,000.

49 Katharinen-Hospital

Amongst the many special clinics and modern institutes the Katharinen-Hospital is probably the most important infirmary in the city. Other important hospitals are the Bürger-Hospital in the Tunzhofer Strasse, the Marien-Hospital in the Böheimstrasse and the Robert-Bosch-Krankenhaus. In total, Stuttgart possesses 7300 hospital beds including the municipal and private hospitals.

50 Freiberg District, Highrise Building

Beyond the Max-Eyth Lake and the northern suburbs of the city one can catch sight of the white blocks of flats in the Freiberg districts. With its 22 storeys the Julius Brecht House is still the largest high block of flats in the Federal Republic. As far as size and capacity are concerned its position has been challenged recently by the much discussed building project "Hannibal" in the southern part of the city which is to comprise 1000 owner-occupied flats in up to 15-storey wings.

51 Fasanenhof District, Salute Block of Flats

In the residential area of Fasanenhof, not far from the suburb Degerloch and Möhringen, there is a pleasant interplay of tall buildings and lower groups of houses. About 10,000 people have found a new home here.

52 The River Port of Stuttgart

From the 17th storey of a grain-silo one can gaze down on to the quays with their warehouses and across to the bunkers of the oil and safety harbours. With an area of over 100 hectares the harbour region spreads out between the suburbs of Hedelfingen, Obertürkheim, Untertürkheim, and Wangen. The quays extend for over 3.5 miles and are provided with 18 miles of railway line. About 3 million tons of goods are handled per year which have come from the sea ports in the Channel up the Rhine and Neckar to Stuttgart and Plochingen or, in reverse, are being sent from the Swabian industrial region out to the ports of the world. The water-way Stuttgart–Heilbronn–Mannheim with its 23 locks can be navigated by barges up to 328 feet in length.

53 Stuttgart-Air Port

With a total of over 1.7 million passengers the Stuttgart Airport has become one of the most important traffic intersection points in southern Germany. Over 80,000 aircraft land and take off here each year, including also the largest passenger planes such as the "Jumbo Jet". Of even greater importance than the number of passengers is the share of Stuttgart's airport in the export trade: As far as export air-freight is concerned, Stuttgart is second only to Frankfurt. The value of goods exported by air-freight in 1970 was approx. 1 million DM.

54 At the Killesberg Gardens

The extensive and elevated Killesberg Park with its fountains and lawns, exhibition halls and restaurants offers Stuttgart and the city's guests unique recreation facilities. It is a garden and exhibition ground all rolled into one and although it is high above the city it can be reached in 10 minutes from the centre. Since the first post-war Horticultural Show took place in 1950, it has constantly been improved and extended. Plans have been drawn up to expand the existing area and thus decisively improve the space for exhibitions.

55 The Wilhelma Zoo Gardens

The Stuttgart "Wilhelma" occupies a special position amongst the German zoological and botanical gardens. On the grounds of a former royal pleasure gardens — with a little castle in Moorish style — arose the only biological garden in the Federal Republic with an aquarium which is the largest in Europe. Greenhouses for cacti and palms, the open-air enclosures for sea lions and sea elephants, the new quarters for beasts of prey, the elephant house and also the aquarium show are the points of greatest attraction in these large gardens.

56/ 57 The River Neckar with Rosenstein Castle

Rosenstein Castle is situated on a hill and has a grand view over the Neckar and Bad Cannstatt on the opposite site. King Wilhelm I commissioned the Florentine architect Salucci to construct the building in classical style between 1825–1829. Today it houses the collection of the State Museum for natural science. Beneath the castle the white motor-ships of the "Neckarflotte" are lying at anchor; in the summer season they make daily trips down river as far as Heilbronn or up river for sight-seeing in the harbour.

58 Leuze Mineral Baths

Near to the banks of the Neckar, mineral springs exist which have medicinal powers, and on warm summer days are a meeting point for tens of thousands of Stuttgart citizens. In the Leuze mineral baths over 790 gallons of mineral water are pumped in per minute, and thus the water in the swimming-pool and indoor baths is constantly kept fresh. In the nearby Berg

Mineral Baths the half-acre mineral water swimming-pool is situated amidst green lawns and trees. A new Assembly-room (pump room) was built in Leuze in 1965 and offers a wide range of modern medicinal cures.

59 Bad Cannstatt, the Spa Room

The tradition of the baths in Cannstatt dates back to the time of the Romans. At the beginning of the 19th century the two main springs, "das Männlein und das Weiblein", were planned in a new way in the so-called "Badgarten". Since then Bad Cannstatt has not looked back. It is visited by an increasing number of German and foreign visitors, and each year undergoes modern improvement. Apart from the medicinal and mineral baths the assembly-room offers space and facilities for festivities and functions of all kinds.

60 View to Bad Cannstatt

Bad Cannstatt, which was formerly an independent town, is one of the most charming regions of "Old Stuttgart". Quite a number of the typical Swabian houses from previous centuries have been preserved in the streets. Especially during the wine festival, when the citizens of Cannstatt sit down together on the open street over a glass of wine and a "Laugenbretzel" and have a good time, might one think that the clock had been turned back to more tranquil times. In the background can be seen the steeple of the town church, with the particularly interesting dome which Heinrich Schickhardt designed.

61 Daimler-Benz Museum

More than a hundred years ago, in Bad Cannstatt as well as simultaneously in Mannheim, the history of the automobile began. Together with his chief designer Maybach Gottlieb Daimler created out of a coach the first motor car and Karl Benz constructed his first "Patent-Motor-Car". A selection of historical vehicles from the Daimler motorcycle of 1885 up to the streamlined racing cars is exhibited in the Daimler-Benz Museum in Stuttgart-Untertürkheim. Since its inauguration over 2 million visitors have come to gaze at the forerunners of the modern car and "oldtimers".

62 Cannstatt Fun Fair

Every year in autumn Stuttgarter and Swabians from all over the world come together for the Cannstatt Fair "Auf dem Wasen". It was inaugurated in 1818 by King Wilhelm I of Wurtemberg. The 78-foot-high "Fruchtsäule" (fruit tower), a symbol of the original meaning of this agricultural fair, looks down on the bustle of the gay streets and beer tents, the switchback and the merry-go-round. Amongst the three million visitors one might come across American Swabians who have come all this way by charted planes in order to be present at the "Cannstatt Wasen".

63 View from Uhlbach on the Rotenberg

The fertile slopes of the vineyards are just as much part of the Stuttgart image as the peaceful composure of the little villages in the green outskirts. Above Uhlbach with its quaint timber-framed Town Hall one can ascend through vineyards to the Rotenberg where there is a chapel in which King Wilhelm I and his wife are buried. The view from the Rotenberg across the Neckar valley is one of the most beautiful which Stuttgart has to offer.

64 Solitude Palace

The little white Roccoco palace not far from Leonberg was commissioned by the Herzog Karl Eugen between 1763–1767 and was intended to serve as a place of "solitude" in the sense of the expression at that time: with dancing and hunting, sociability and summer feasts. Today the "Solitude" is one of the most favourite excursion points around Stuttgart.

Index

18/19   Stadtzentrum, vom Eugensplatz aus gesehen · The City Centre · Vue du centre de la ville
◁   Am Fernsehturm · The Television Tower · La tour de télévision

20   Am Alten Schloß · The Old Castle · Le vieux château

21   Schillerplatz mit Stiftskirche · Schiller Square and Collegiate Church · La place Schiller ▷

23   Innenhof des Alten Schlosses · Courtyard of the Old Castle · Cour intérieure du vieux c

24/25   Schloßplatz mit den Türmen der Stadt · Schlossplatz with Towers of the Town · Schlossplatz

27   Markt und Stiftskirche · Market square with Collegiate Church · La place du marché

◁   Kreuzigungsgruppe an der Leonhardskirche · Crucifix at Leonhard Church · Crucifix à St-Léonard

28   Blumenmarkt und Rathausturm · Flower's Market and Town Hall · Le marché des fleurs, l'hôtel de ville

29   In der Schulstraße · View of Schulstrasse · Dans la Schulstrasse

31   Café am Kleinen Schloßplatz · Café at "Kleiner Schlossplatz" · «Kleiner Schlossplatz», au café

◁   Kleiner Schloßplatz · New City Centre, called "Kleiner Schlossplatz" · «Kleiner Schlossplatz»

33 Staatstheater, Großes Haus mit Theatersee · The Opera House with Theatre Pond · L'opéra
◁ Königsbau am Schloßplatz · "Königsbau" in the Castle Square · L'immeuble «Königsbau»

34   Neues Schloß, Mittelbau · The New Castle, Inner Courtyard · Cour intérieure du nouveau château

35 Schloßgarten mit Neuem Schloß · At the New Castle · Au nouveau château

36   Staatstheater, Kleines Haus · Small House of the State Theatre · Le théatre («Kleines Haus»)

37   Wasserspiele im Schloßgarten · Fountains at the Castle Gardens · Les fontaines au jardin du château

39   Kreuzungsbauwerk Charlottenplatz · Cross-Roads Charlottenplatz · Charlottenplatz

◁   Königstraße mit Bahnhofsturm · Königstrasse and Main Station · La Königstrasse, la Gare Centrale

40/41　U-Bahnhof Charlottenplatz · Charlottenplatz, Underground Tramway · Station «Charlottenplatz»

42   Friedrichstraße · Office Buildings at the Friedrichstrasse · Immeubles modernes, Friedrichstrasse

43   Hofbräueck und Tagblatt-Turm · Hofbräu Corner, Tagblatt Skyscraper · La tour du journal

44/45   An der Liederhalle · In front of the Concert Hall · Liederhalle

46 Kollegiengebäude der Universität · College Buildings of the University · Bâtiments des facultés

47   Universitäts-Neubauten am Pfaffenwald · The New University, Pfaffenwald · L'université nouvelle

48 Gottlieb-Daimler-Gymnasium, Bad Cannstatt · Gottlieb Daimler High School · Lycée Gottlieb-Daimler

49   Katharinen-Hospital · Modern Hospital "Katharinen-Hospital" · L'hôpital «Katharinen-Hospital»

50   Hochhaus Julius Brecht, Freiberg · Freiberg District, Highrise Building · Gratte ciel à Freiberg

51 Hochhaus Salute, Fasanenhof · Fasanenhof District, Highrise Building · Gratte ciel «Salute»

52   Blick über den Stuttgarter Hafen · The River Port of Stuttgart · Vue sur le port de Stuttgart

53   Flughafen Stuttgart · Stuttgart Air Port · L'aéroport de Stuttgart

54   Im Höhenpark Killesberg · At the Killesberg Gardens · Aux jardins du Killesberg

55   In der Wilhelma · The Wilhelma Zoo Gardens · Dans la Wilhelma, Jardin Zoologique et Botanique ▷

56/57 Schloß Rosenstein mit der Neckarflotte · Rosenstein Castle · Le château Rosenstein au Neckar

58   Im Mineralbad Leuze · Leuze Mineral Bathes · Les bains minérals de Leuze

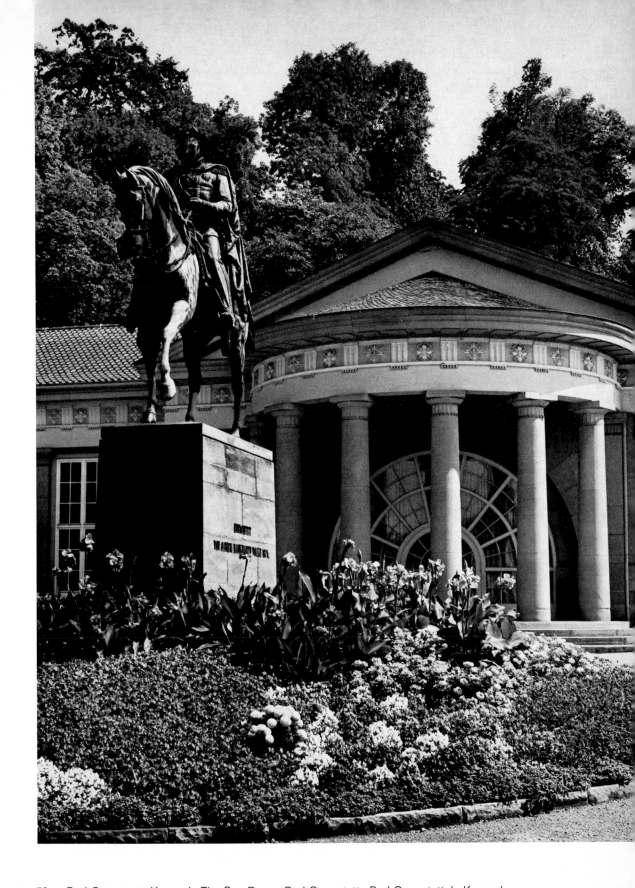

59   Bad Cannstatt: Kursaal · The Spa Room, Bad Cannstatt · Bad Cannstatt, le Kursaal

60   Blick auf Bad Cannstatt am Neckar · View to Bad Cannstatt · Vue sur Bad Cannstatt sur le Neckar

61　Daimler-Benz-Museum · Daimler-Benz Museum · Le musée des autos historiques Daimler-Benz

63   Blick zum Rotenberg · View from Uhlbach on to Rotenberg · Vue d'Uhlbach sur le Rotenberg

◁   Cannstatter Volksfest auf dem Wasen · Fun Fair called "Cannstatter Wasen" · La fête du «Wasen»

64   Schloß Solitude · Solitude Palace · Le petit château Solitude